PUPPY **LOVE**

TRUE STORIES OF DOGGIE DEVOTION

PUPPY **LOVE**

LISA M. GERRY

NATIONAL GEOGRAPHIC
WASHINGTON, D.C.

Chocolate Labrador

Boston terrier

Border collie

Mixed breed

Contents

Introduction

**To be loved by a dog
is an awesome thing.**

Dogs don't care what we wear or if we dance funny. They're not concerned if we got an A or a C on our test or if we struck out during the big game. There's never any reason to feel embarrassed or self-conscious around a dog, because no matter what silly thing you do or say, a dog will love you just the same.

And, even though they sometimes chase their tails, or get their heads stuck in a paper bag looking for that last French fry, there's actually a lot we can learn from our furry friends. Dogs are incredibly loyal—once they love you, you are theirs for life. They also remind us that every day, and in most moments, there are opportunities to have fun. We just have to look for them.

Dogs have an incredible work ethic. When they have a job to do, they are focused, determined, and persistent, and they won't give up until they've achieved their goal. But maybe the best thing about dogs is that when they love you, they're not shy about letting you know. They show you, in big, bold ways, that they're excited to see you (sometimes every time they see you!).

In this book, you will read 25 stories about amazing dogs and the people who love them. With expert help from Dr. Gary Weitzman, president of the San Diego Humane Society and SPCA and cohost of *The Animal House* on public radio, you'll get to the bottom of doggie mysteries like what it might mean when they lick you, why they're so loyal, and whether they really do love us back (spoiler alert: They do!).

You'll meet service dogs that perform important tasks to help their owners live happier, healthier, more fulfilling lives. There are dogs who, when faced with danger, acted quickly and heroically to save the people they love. Some of the dogs in these pages can perform mind-blowing physical feats, things you may not have known a dog could do!

But most of all, the dogs here will inspire you with their courage, unconditional love, and all-around cuteness. Because as anyone who loves them knows, life is just better with a dog.

Dogs are feisty and fun, like this playful border collie, but they can also be your best friend and a treasured part of your family.

Until

by J. Patrick Lewis

Labrador retriever

I want to have a dog beside me until
the last wind blows out the last candle,
until thunder beats lightning
to Earth by a mile, until birds
fly north for the winter.

I want a dog to want me
beside her until the first
petal falls from the last rose,
until someone captures
midnight in a jar,
until summer lets go
of my hand.

Loyal

Dalmatian

MAMA, JAKE, MISHKA, AND STRYDER

♥

OLYMPIC WINNERS
Mixed breeds / Colorado

 Gus Kenworthy is a member of the U.S. freeskiing team. In freeskiing, skiers perform a variety of tricks on both jumps and rails, similar to a skateboarding park on snow. In the 2014 Winter Olympics in Sochi, Russia, Gus competed in the first ever, slope-style skiing event and won a silver medal.

But, when he returned home, he had more than an Olympic victory—he brought with him four new furry friends.

Growing up in Telluride, Colorado, Gus has always loved dogs. So, he was very sad to hear the reports that nearly 2,000

Citizens in Sochi are not encouraged to spay and neuter their dogs, so there are a lot of puppies born without homes and thousands of stray dogs wandering the streets.

stray dogs in the Russian city were going to be put down in the months before the Olympics.

Once he got to Sochi, Gus saw lots of dogs wandering the streets. Then, one day, he got a call from his best friend, Robin Macdonald, a photographer who was also in the Olympic Village. Robin had discovered five stray dogs—a mom and her four pups—in a tent allocated for members of the media.

When Robin brought Gus to meet the dogs, he was surprised to find that they didn't seem wild or skittish. Instead, they were incredibly friendly and snuggly. Every day after he finished his training, Gus would meet Robin and take a bus to see the dogs. They would feed them and play with them. Gus fell in love right away and he knew he had to help them.

When Gus posted a photo of himself with the four puppies on Instagram and Twitter, he immediately began receiving thousands of likes and retweets. Everyone, it seemed, wanted to know more about the sweet Sochi pups.

Gus decided that he was going to do everything he could to bring the dogs back home with him, especially after one of them went missing. Right away, friends and family back in the United States started calling dibs on the dogs. Many people were willing and eager to give them happy homes.

Gus and Robin began arranging for crates, passports for the dogs, and getting all the required vaccinations to bring the dogs on the plane and take them home to the United States. When other obligations forced Gus to head back to the U.S. before the dogs could leave, Robin stayed behind with them.

ASK AN **EXPERT**

Q: Why are dogs so loyal to humans? Is it because they know that if they stick with us they'll get fed?

Dr. Weitzman: Loyalty is one of the best traits that dogs have. For a lot of dogs, food is secondary to the attention we give them. Some dogs are a one-person dog and they'll be loyal to that person forever. Other dogs are loyal to a group, or their pack, which may include multiple humans.

Dogs' loyalty to people is one of the main reasons humans domesticated them nearly 30,000 years ago.

HEROIC HOUNDS

When someone is missing or there's been a disaster, often search-and-rescue teams will use dogs (and their powerful sense of smell!) to help find people. Some dogs are trained to sniff out any humans in the area, whereas trailing dogs are trained to locate a specific person's scent. Though dogs from any breed can be great at search and rescue, the ones most often used are herding and sporting dogs, like German shepherds, border collies, golden retrievers, and Labrador retrievers. Here's why: It's important that these heroic dogs are driven to succeed at a specific goal. When you're looking for a missing person, you don't want a dog that is happy to give up and lie down. Also, they must work well with a handler and be physically strong, very smart, and highly trainable.

It took another month for Robin and the Humane Society International to convince the Russian government to let him take the dogs.

Then, sadly, Robin wasn't allowed to take two of the puppies to get the medical attention they needed, and they died before he could get them help.

Eventually, though, Robin boarded a plane home with Mama, her puppy Jake, and two other stray puppies, Mishka and Stryder. When they arrived in the U.S., it took them a little while to adjust to the time difference—and to be

Kelli Stack, a forward on the U.S. women's hockey team, Olympic snowboarder Lindsey Jacobellis, and actress Katherine Heigl were among those who adopted dogs from Sochi and brought them back to the United States.

house-trained!—but with all of the healthy meals, love, and snuggles they were receiving, the dogs were on their way to being happy and healthy.

Mama is now living with Gus's mom, Jake and Mishka are with Gus and Robin, and a woman who works for the Humane Society International adopted Stryder.

Gus may have won a silver medal in the 2014 Winter Olympic games, but it was when he rescued these four adorable dogs from across the world that he proved he has a heart of gold.

LUCY

♥

EMERGENCY RESPONDER

Husky-beagle mix / Massachusetts

The day started just like any other. John Miles and his dog, Lucy, set out for their morning walk, just after 10 a.m. It was only a few days before Thanksgiving and it was already quite cold in Boston.

As John and Lucy walked their normal two-and-a-half-mile (4-km) route, John decided to cross to the other side of the street, where the sun was shining. So, he waited for the cars to pass and then he stepped off of the curb—and that's the last thing John remembers about that day.

Eight years earlier, John's son and daughter had rescued

Microchips, implanted under your dog's skin, have a unique identification number that can be used to look up your family's contact information.

Lucy from a local shelter and gave the pup to their dad as a Father's Day present. Now it was Lucy's turn to do the rescuing. And that's exactly what she did.

Right after John started to cross the street, he and Lucy were hit by a car. John suffered serious injuries and was unable to move, but Lucy immediately sprang into action. Even though she'd torn cartilage in her knee during the accident, she pushed through the pain and limped to a nearby dentist's office. She stood outside and began barking feverishly.

The office staff heard the crash and when Lucy began barking, they rushed outside. Lucy then led them to John and they immediately called 911. Then, Lucy sat next to John and wouldn't leave his side until the ambulance arrived.

John hadn't brought his phone or any identification with him on their walk, but thankfully, Lucy was wearing her collar tags. When animal control arrived along with the emergency responders, they were able to identify John and contact his wife, Katy.

John suffered tremendous injuries. He had 55 total fractures, including many in his face, four broken toes, a broken ankle, and two broken bones in his lower leg. He received 70 facial stitches and also had to have his entire shoulder replaced.

Lucy had to have surgery on her knee, but worse for her, it seemed, was being away from her beloved owner. While he was in

Seeing Lucy in the hospital, and talking about her heroics, helped to lift John's spirits.

the hospital, she would limp around the house to each of John's favorite spots, then stand at the front door and cry.

As soon as John was moved from the intensive care unit to a regular room, his family was able to bring Lucy to visit him. It was an emotional reunion and when Lucy saw John, she ran right over to the bed and was happier and more energetic than she had been since the accident.

Katy always knew Lucy was smart and John always knew Lucy was strong—the two of them would walk a total of five miles (8 km) together every day. But on that November day, Lucy proved one more thing John and Katy had suspected all along—they had one incredibly special dog.

HENRY

♥

THE ART OF THE SAVE

Labrador retriever / Tennessee

Frank Walker was pleasantly surprised when he stepped out onto his large property in Tennessee. Even though it was February, and technically still winter, the weather was warm enough to work outside. Frank had been eagerly waiting for an opportunity to cut down the dead tree behind his house—and today was the day.

Henry, Frank's chocolate Labrador retriever, remained by his side as he began the job. For more than ten years, Henry has been Frank's constant and loyal companion. When Frank rides in his golf cart or drives his car, Henry sits in the seat next to him. Frank trained Henry to stay in the yard—without the need for a fence! Henry even stays close by at night, curled up at the foot of Frank's bed.

But on this day, Henry did far more than just keep Frank company. On this day, Henry saved Frank's life.

As Frank prepared for an afternoon of chopping, he set his coat down nearby to enjoy the fresh air. Although cutting down the tree was tough work, Frank was used to this sort of labor. After chopping away the dead wood, the tree started to fall and Frank waited for its satisfying crash to the ground.

But instead of falling away from him, as it was meant to, the tree fell toward Frank and pinned him against the ground! Frank could tell right away that he'd broken his ribs and badly injured his legs. "My arms and legs were twisted like a pretzel," said Frank.

HEALTHY HOUNDS

Dogs are incredibly intuitive, observant, and have superpowerful sniffers. Sometimes, these traits make it possible for them to pick up on medical issues before humans do. They notice behavior changes that are out of the ordinary, they sense when you're distressed, and they also can smell things that humans cannot. One amazing example of this is how service dogs can detect blood sugar changes for diabetic owners. These dogs are trained to identify a particular smell on their owner's breath that occurs when their blood sugar levels drop quickly or get too low. The dog then alerts their owner, by nudging them or pawing them, to let them know that they need to check their blood sugar levels immediately, or get something to eat. The dog can also be trained to get help or retrieve juice or glucose tabs to help raise their owner's blood sugar.

Henry was startled to see his owner in pain. Frank wasn't able to move, or even scream. He had brought his cell phone with him outside, but it was in the pocket of his coat, which he'd taken off earlier and was sitting beyond his reach.

For three long hours, Frank was stuck beneath the tree, slowly weakening and fighting to stay conscious. Henry stayed by his side the entire time, licking his face and barking to keep him warm and alert.

"I was doing a lot of praying and thinking about ways I was going to survive," said Frank. Then, all of a sudden, even though Henry had been trained not leave the property on his own, the loyal lab made a mad dash from the house.

It was Henry's smart, brave decision to run that ultimately saved Frank's life.

Henry ran out of the yard and toward a man who had just recently moved to the neighborhood. Thankfully, when Frank had introduced Henry to the man a month before, Frank had said, "If you see Henry without me, you'll know something is wrong."

Henry ran to the man and began frantically barking. At first, not knowing what Henry was trying to tell him, the neighbor didn't respond. But when Henry raced toward him a second time and continued to bark, his strange behavior caused the man to recall Frank's words and realize something was very wrong. Finally, he followed the dog back to where Frank was lying helpless under the tree.

The neighbor called for help and after more than ten hours of surgery for his many broken bones and other injuries, Frank was in stable condition. When Frank was released from the hospital, he and his wife rewarded Henry for his smart thinking and bravery.

"We got him lots of treats," said Frank. "And we give him a *lot* of love. He's my godsend."

ASK AN **EXPERT**

Q: Why are dogs so smart?

Dr. Weitzman: Being dog smart is different from being people smart. Dogs are street-smart and have excellent intuition. They're great at recognizing faces, as well as reading body language and tone of voice. In fact, I wish that more people were as "smart" as dogs. But even among dogs, some are definitely more intelligent than others, and there are even certain breeds we think of as "smart dogs," such as border collies and Australian shepherds. But be warned: Sometimes the smartest dogs can be the most difficult to have as a pet!

ANGEL

♥

COURAGEOUS CANINE

Golden retriever / Canada

It was getting close to dinnertime when 11-year-old Austin Forman trudged outside to collect firewood in his snowy backyard, in Boston Bar, British Columbia, Canada. As always, his best friend and golden retriever, Angel, tagged along. But unlike most days, instead of running around and playing in the yard, Angel was acting strange.

She was following Austin closely, sticking much closer to him than usual. Austin thought Angel was just being sweet. But it turns out, Angel had already detected danger nearby.

A cougar is a member of the cat family and also goes by the names mountain lion, puma, or catamount.

Austin continued loading logs into a wheelbarrow, but then something caught his eye—something Angel had already seen. There was another animal in the backyard. At first, Austin thought it was probably another dog. But when it walked beneath a nearby light, Austin recognized the dangerous predator. It was a cougar.

Cougars usually hunt at dusk for animals like deer, coyotes, and raccoons. But this cougar, it seemed, had set his sights on young Austin.

Before Austin could run, or even scream, the cougar lunged at him, trying to attack. Just as the cougar made its move, Angel put her life at risk, stepping between Austin and the cougar. The cougar mauled Angel's head, wrestled her to the ground, and dragged her under the porch.

Because of Angel's brave sacrifice, Austin had the chance to run safely into his house and tell his mom what had happened. Austin's mom called the Royal Canadian Mounted Police, and luckily, Constable Chad Gravelle was close by when he received the call.

When the constable arrived on the scene, Angel and the cougar were tangled together, fighting under the porch. The constable drew his gun, but was scared that he might not be able to shoot the cougar without accidentally shooting Angel. When he has able to get a clear shot, he fired twice, killing the cougar.

At first, Angel was motionless when they pulled the cougar off her body. Austin and his family feared the worst. But all at once, Angel took a deep breath, jumped up, and shook her fur. She was alive!

Despite the fact that she had just narrowly escaped death, she immediately ran to Austin to make sure he was unharmed. She gave him a good sniff and checked that he was all in one piece. The family knows that nothing, even if it's dangerous and risky, could stop Angel from protecting her best friend.

Angel did suffer some serious injuries and needed surgery. But today, except for a few scars, she has fully recovered. To welcome her home from the vet, Austin bought Angel her favorite treat—a big, juicy steak. It was the least he could do to say thanks to Angel, his best friend and the hero who saved his life.

JAROD

♥

A FEARLESS FRIEND

Chow Chow / Canada

It was a crisp fall day in Genelle, British Columbia, Canada, and the sun was beginning to set in Donna Perreault's backyard. She was talking on the phone with her son, while her dog Meesha was playing out in the backyard. Her other dog, Jarod, was with her inside the house.

Jarod and Meesha are both chow chows, a breed known for their protective nature. Jarod was a rescue. Donna adopted him from a shelter when he was six years old, saving him from almost certain death. Little did Donna know that he would soon do the same for her.

> **Because the day was so windy,
> and bears rely heavily on their sense of smell,
> it may not have known Meesha was there
> until it heard her.**

Suddenly, the ordinary moment turned to terror when Donna heard Meesha sound a warning bark. Donna turned to look out the window and witnessed a dark shadowy figure lumbering toward Meesha. She couldn't quite make out what it was, but at that size, there was only one possibility: Meesha was face-to-face with a black bear. Alarmed by the noise of Meesha's sharp bark, the bear lunged to attack.

Donna threw down the phone and ran outside, hoping to distract the bear away from Meesha. But Jarod had another idea. He burst through the back door and dashed toward Donna. What happened next made him a hero …

When Donna ran out, the bear began to retreat, but Meesha chased it. Jarod jumped in to defend his owner and his sister, and the bear angrily turned from one dog to the other. Helpless to defend her pups, Donna picked up a mop bucket and hit the bear on its rear end. The bear, infuriated, charged at Donna, backing her up against the garage door.

Terrified, Donna tried to defend herself with a mop, but the bear continued to pursue her. In one final attempt to save her own life, Donna hit the bear right on the nose. Stunned, the bear paused and shook his head. Jarod seized this moment of distraction and pounced onto the bear's back, biting down hard. The bear turned away from Donna, giving her and Meesha enough time to run inside while Jarod played decoy and lured the bear around the other side of the house. For a few minutes, Donna thought the worst. Then, a few moments later, Jarod ran inside. The bear was nowhere in sight!

During the attack, Meesha and Jarod were a bit banged up but neither was seriously hurt. Donna saw the doctor to treat some wounds she sustained from the bear clawing at her, but overall, she was relieved to be alive and grateful to her heroic pet.

"Jarod was so happy to know we were all fine," said Donna. "Now, when we go on walks, he never lets me out of his sight."

Chow Chow

ORIGIN: China

COLOR(S): Red, black, blue, cinnamon, and cream

HEIGHT: 17 to 20 inches (43 to 51 cm)

TEMPERAMENT: Very loyal, intelligent, independent, naturally protective, and reserved

THE LOYAL ONES

SUPER SERVICE DOGS

The **Warrior Canine Connection (WCC)** is an organization where military veterans train service dogs for other veterans who need them. **Molly Morelli,** director of dog programs for the WCC, shares what these amazing dogs can do and how they're helping.

Q: What exactly does the WCC do?
A: A certified trainer teaches wounded warriors with post-traumatic stress disorder (PTSD) and/or traumatic brain injury how to train service dogs for veterans with mobility impairments. The training itself has been proven to be very therapeutic.

Q: What are some of the things you train dogs to do?
A: Retrieving dropped items is probably the command used most often. We teach the dogs to turn lights on and off, tug open doors, and pull wheelchairs. We teach them to provide balance for someone, such as an amputee who is learning to walk with their prosthetics. For people with PTSD, we train the dogs to recognize and interrupt high stress behaviors, like covering their face with their hands or shaking their leg. We'll also train dogs to wake them up when they're having nightmares.

The WCC breeds golden retrievers and Labrador puppies—like this adorable Labrador retriever puppy from a recent litter—because of their even temperament.

Q: How early do you begin training the dogs?

A: Really from the moment they're born. We hold them and touch them, and every day they get visitors to help socialize them. Then, when they're four or five weeks old, and they're up moving around, we start introducing simple commands to teach them how to do something right, before they learn how to do it wrong.

Q: Can you give an example of a command and how you would train the dog to follow it?

A: For every single command, we teach the dogs bit by bit. For example, to teach a dog to turn on a light, we start with a small handheld light switch. Then we progress to a switch that's on a board, placed lower on the wall. Finally, we actually have them flip the switch up on the wall. It's all done in increments.

Q: How have you seen veterans benefit from their dogs?

A: One of the biggest things that we see is better sleep. Sleep is one of the biggest issues that we see in the population we work with, and you really can't function if you don't get a good night's sleep. But when the veterans get the chance to take a dog home, all of a sudden they're sleeping. Recently, there was a guy who was only sleeping, on average, a half hour every night. Then, the first night he took a dog home, he slept six hours straight.

Q: Why do you think dogs make such great service animals?

A: Dogs love unconditionally and they just want to please you. They don't get frustrated when you drop the same thing ten times in a day. Whereas a human caregiver might get frustrated, a golden retriever is going to pick it up for you every time you need them to without question.

SUPERCUTE **ALERT**

Check out the Warrior Canine Connection's puppy cam on Explore.org. You can watch new litters of adorable puppies eating, sleeping, and, of course, playing!

Beagle

WILLOW

♥

A WAY WITH WORDS

Terrier mix / New York

 Little Willow, a brown, black, and white terrier mix, sits up on her hind legs with her front paws pulled up to her chest. Then, she drops down to all fours and raises just one of her front paws to say, "Hello." Last, she flops over on her back and plays dead. These tricks are pretty impressive all on their own, but they're even more amazing when you find out how Willow receives the commands: She *reads* them.

Unlike most dogs, who follow spoken, or audible, commands, Willow reads, "Sit up," "Wave," and "Bang," which

> If you tell her to, Willow can control her volume and will bark either loudly or softly. **She can stop wagging her tail, crawl, and even sneeze on command.**

are written on pieces of paper. When Willow sees the word "Bang," she rolls over on her back to pretend she's been shot. Willow's owner, Lyssa Howells, is a dog trainer and was looking for a new challenge for her smart pup. Willow had already learned to ride a horse and skateboard! And, she was able to follow almost 250 spoken commands.

To teach Willow how to read commands, Lyssa first taught her to do the tricks when the words were spoken aloud. When Willow would respond correctly, she would get a treat. Then, Lyssa would hold up the signs while speaking the words, so that Willow would connect seeing the word with hearing it. Finally, within six weeks, Willow could respond to the written cues without hearing them at all. "It's repetition, just like anything," said Lyssa. "She learned to understand that particular order of letters, whether they were handwritten or typed."

Willow goes everywhere with her owner, even to training sessions for other dogs. If Lyssa is trying to teach another dog to sit or stay, she sometimes uses Willow as a distraction so that the other dog can practice following a command, even when tempted to play.

"She's just really brilliant," said Lyssa. Willow has a number of ways of communicating to Lyssa. For example, when Willow is hungry, she tells Lyssa by putting her paw on her food bowl. If Lyssa says, "Can you please go to the kitchen and grab me a pen?" Willow knows exactly what to do and will go retrieve the pen.

Willow can understand the order of letters, whether they are handwritten or typed!

Another cool trick Willow can do is "count." Lyssa will hold different amounts of rocks, pennies, or treats in each of her hands. Then, she asks Willow which hand has more in it or less in it and Willow will put her paw on the correct hand. Pretty amazing! Now, if only we could train dogs to help with our homework.

EVER WONDERED...

what your funny four-legged friend was trying to tell you? Well, wonder no more. Here we translate some top doggie behaviors so you and your canine companion can get to know each other better!

LICKING

This behavior evolved from when mother wolves fed their pups from their mouths, just like baby birds. But today when a dog licks you, it most likely means they like you and accept you.

WHINING

Whining usually means the dog is uncomfortable or in pain, or it wants something.

BARKING

Barking is a way of communicating, and different sounding barks mean different things. For example, a high-pitched bark might mean the dog is alarmed or is trying to warn you about something. A low growl bark is a warning that the dog might be feeling aggressive and you should back away.

K'OS

♥

SAFETY PATROL

Neapolitan mastiff / Canada

 Intelligence shows itself in various ways— sometimes through persistence and determination.

That's exactly what this big Neapolitan mastiff showed late one night, when his family was asleep.

Jason and Linda Guindon were sleeping soundly, when K'os (pronounced like the word "chaos") jumped onto their bed, barking. Knowing him to be a calm, quiet dog, they knew instantly that something big must be wrong.

Jason ran downstairs, afraid someone might have broken into the house, but that didn't calm K'os. The Guindons knew their pup was trying to tell them something, but at first, they weren't sure what. The smart dog kept running back and forth between Jason and Linda's room and their son Hunter's room down the hall, barking all the while.

Linda followed K'os into Hunter's room, and she realized what K'os had been trying show them—their son was having a seizure and was also choking. Immediately, Linda turned Hunter on his side and cleared his airway so that he could breathe while Jason called for help.

K'os laid beside Hunter to comfort him, and he remained there until the ambulance arrived. Hunter doesn't remember having the seizure, but he does remember waking up to the paramedics standing over him and K'os lying beside him.

Neapolitan mastiff is a breed known for being loyal and protective, but Jason and Linda could never have imagined that their good-natured pup would save their son's life. In fact, they had thought that every single night the dog was spending the whole night fast asleep at the foot of their bed. But, it turns out, this pup had been sneaking out during the wee hours, routinely checking in on each room. K'os had been watching out for the family all along.

A few months after the first incident, unfortunately, Hunter suffered another seizure. Once again, K'os alerted his parents to what was happening. Hunter was diagnosed with epilepsy and doctors were able to perform surgery on his brain to prevent future seizures.

Nonetheless, K'os continues to protect Hunter. "I can hear him come in all the time at night," he said. "Sometimes I will see him poke the door open and check on me."

Jason, too, has gotten used to his pup's nightly routine. "K'os normally sleeps on our bed, but several times a night I will hear him go down the hall, check in on Hunter, and then come back," he said.

As for K'os, he continues to be an important and celebrated part of the family. Jason had named him "K'os" because he thought having such a big dog would bring excitement and a bit of disorder to their lives. That was hardly the case.

"Instead, he has brought a calm, comforting peacefulness to our family," said Jason. "He's literally everyone's best friend. He's simply perfect."

HATTIE

♥

EARS ON ALERT
Labrador retriever / Pennsylvania

Jennifer Warsing lost her hearing when she was just five years old. But when she began living alone as an adult, she struggled with several day-to-day activities. On top of that, her life was becoming filled with fear.

Jennifer loved cooking, but it was difficult for her. She would often burn the food she tried to bake because she couldn't hear the timer go off in the kitchen.

Living alone was sometimes scary because Jennifer knew if she were ever in danger, she wouldn't be able to hear the warnings. She wouldn't hear someone break into her house,

> **For 23 years in a row, the Labrador retriever topped the American Kennel Club's list of most popular breeds.**

and if there were a fire, she wouldn't hear the alarm. She felt even more vulnerable outside, where she wasn't able to hear what was going on around her.

But all of that changed when she met Hattie, a chocolate Labrador retriever. Hattie was found in a shelter and adopted by the organization Dogs for the Deaf. For eight months she was trained to help people with disabilities, specifically someone with a hearing impairment. Hattie was paired with Jennifer, having proven herself a very wise and smart dog.

When Hattie entered Jennifer's life, many things that had once seemed impossible were now within reach. "After Hattie's arrival, I cooked an entire Thanksgiving meal for my family, and I've done it every year since," said Jennifer.

Hearing dogs are taught to alert their owner to household sounds that are important to their safety. Hattie alerts Jennifer—by nudging her with her nose—to let her know when the doorbell rings, if there's a child crying nearby, when the phone rings, or if the timer in the kitchen goes off.

Hattie is caring and smart, so she's even able to anticipate danger and alert Jennifer before it happens—even in situations she has not been expressly trained for. On one occasion, Hattie continually nudged Jennifer while she was working on her computer. Jennifer wasn't sure what Hattie was trying to tell her, so she kept working.

Hattie helps her owner, who's hearing-impaired, live a fuller, less fearful life.

Then, Hattie pressed her body against Jennifer, pinning her against the desk so that she couldn't get up. That's when the ground beneath them began moving like a rolling wave. They were feeling the aftershocks of an earthquake that had hit a neighboring state. Hattie had sensed there was danger and kept Jennifer secure and safe in her seat.

Hattie is such an important part of Jennifer's life that her husband even asked for the pup's approval before he proposed. When Hattie let out a happy, *"Awrrrrooooo!!!!!,"* Jennifer took it as a "Yes!"

Hattie is more than a service dog, she is an answer to Jennifer's prayers. She said, "We are all a match made in heaven."

YOU MIGHT THINK...

you know just what your adorable furball Fido is trying to tell you when he jumps on you, yawns, or wags his tail. But sometimes a canine's conduct doesn't mean what we think it does. Here's what he might really be saying ...

JUMPING

Most dogs are incredible athletes and skilled jumpers, but jumping on people when they come in the door is a really bad habit. It's best to train dogs not to do that. But the reason they do it is that they want to get as close to you, and your face, as possible.

YAWNING

They could be tired, or they could be nervous. Dogs yawn when they're stressed.

TAIL WAGGING

Dogs do this for all different reasons, and you can tell a lot by how fast and how high they're wagging their tails. But it's important to remember that not all wagging tails are happy tails. Dogs will also wag their tails when they're nervous or as a sort of warning.

CHARLIE BOY

♥

TO PROTECT AND SERVE

German shepherd / California

The big, beautiful German shepherd walks just slightly ahead of his owner, Sgt. Major Jesse Acosta. Then, the dog slows down, signaling that there's something in the pair's path. Jesse puts his hand out in front of him, and then feels above his head, trying to detect what it is that Charlie Boy sees.

When he doesn't feel anything, Jesse gives the command, "Go around." Charlie Boy then leads him around whatever obstacle is in their way, whether it be a low-hanging branch, a pothole, or a puddle. When the dog reaches the end of the sidewalk, he stops, a signal for Jesse to stop as well.

For seven years now, Jesse has relied on Charlie Boy to alert him to danger, steer him toward safety, and communicate what he sees. While serving in Iraq in 2006, Jesse was blinded by a bomb explosion. When he returned home, he had to begin adjusting to life without his sight. As soon as he was eligible, Jesse began looking into adopting a guide dog.

Jesse was familiar with German shepherds because of their involvement in the army. Some of them were even brought into combat with the troops. Though it's not always possible to choose what type of dog you get, Jesse had his heart set on a German shepherd.

"I had seen those dogs in action," said Jesse. "They're very intelligent, fast, and loyal." When The Seeing Eye school told him his new dog would be a German shepherd, Jesse was overwhelmed with emotion.

Jesse and Charlie Boy spent 30 days in training, learning how to work together. The first commands that Charlie Boy learned were "left," "right," and "forward." Little by little, he mastered more advanced commands. Today, he recognizes others, such as "back up" or "go around."

Just like other German shepherds, Charlie Boy is very vocal. To let Jesse know there's a dog nearby, he'll start "talking," or barking. If he calms down and starts to wag his tail, Jesse knows that the situation isn't dangerous and there's no need for concern. But, if there is a loose dog without a leash, Charlie Boy will stand in front of Jesse in case the dog is aggressive.

Having Charlie Boy at his side makes Jesse feel more confident and calm. Before Jesse had his canine companion, it was frightening for him just to think about taking a walk down the street. But now, they're a team and they've explored beyond the neighborhood and throughout the country. They've even been guests at the White House!

Charlie Boy can tell when his owner is experiencing symptoms of post-traumatic stress disorder (PTSD) and will nudge Jesse in the face or the hand to remind him that he's not alone and to help calm him. Charlie Boy accompanies Jesse to work every day and even has a special bed underneath the desk.

"He's comforting to me," said Jesse, who gets antsy when he's not around. "When he's there, he soothes me."

It doesn't take long to fall in love with Charlie Boy. Once, Jesse gave a presentation at a school and by the end, the crowd was chanting, "Charlie! Charlie!"

SAY WHAT?

Did you know that if your dog is scratching, it doesn't always mean he has an itch? In fact, scratching might mean your precious pup is feeling nervous. Check out these three other doggie behaviors and what they might mean.

ROLLING ON THEIR BACK

When a dog rolls over and shows you their belly, it means, *You have nothing to worry about from me, I trust you.*

HOWLING

Howling is not meant as a threat. It's just a way that many breeds communicate. Beagles are the howling kings and huskies are also really good at it. Ever hear your dog howl at a fire truck? Because some emergency vehicles sound similar to a howling dog, when dogs hear one, they'll often howl back at them.

RAISING HACKLES

When a dog lifts the hair that runs down their backs, it's similar to when the hair stands up on a person's arm. It means the dog is either scared, alert, or dangerous. Dogs generally do this as a way of communicating with other dogs.

WENDY

♥

QUICK THINKING IN A CRISIS
Labradoodle / Texas

 As a service dog, there are lots of ways that Wendy is trained to help her owner, Richard Heath. But on the day that Richard needed her most, the large, ebony Labradoodle rescued him using intelligence and intuition that no trainer could ever teach.

When Wendy first met Richard, he was in very poor health and suffering from a number of illnesses. His wife, Elaine, thought having a dog around to keep him company would be helpful. Her instincts were spot on.

Wendy and Richard had an immediate connection. The

Studies have found that dogs are good for your health. They help lower blood pressure, decrease your risk of heart disease, **and make you happier!**

first time the dog saw her new owner, she walked right up to him and laid her head in his lap. "They were made for each other," said Elaine.

Right away, caring for Wendy inspired Richard to be more active. Before, Richard spent most of his days inactive and sitting in his chair. But now, Richard had to feed Wendy and let her outside. When Richard was ready to stand, he and Wendy would each hold one end of a tug rope and, as a team, lift him from the chair. If he began to lose his balance, Wendy would push against him to keep him steady.

Wendy is very observant and always watches for new ways to help Richard. For example, he has diabetes and Wendy has learned to alert him when his blood sugar levels are too high or low. She even helps him to do laundry by picking up clothes he drops on the floor and putting them in the dryer.

But this amazing dog did more than simply improve Richard's life. With one quick-thinking act, she saved it.

It was a summer day in Texas, and Richard was working on his computer. Suddenly, he suffered a stroke and collapsed on the floor. Wendy immediately sprang into action. She dragged her owner into the next room and helped him climb into his chair.

Then, she ran and found the phone and brought it back to him. Wendy first placed it in his right hand, but the stroke had paralyzed the right side of his body. Amazingly, Wendy realized this and placed the phone in his other hand. Now, he was able to call Elaine for help.

When Elaine took her husband to the hospital, she made the mistake of leaving Wendy at home. When she returned to the house two hours later, Wendy was beside herself, wanting to be at Richard's side to make sure he was safe.

Elaine brought the loyal pooch back to the hospital to see her owner. She didn't even have to show Wendy the way to Richard's room. Upon entering the hospital, Wendy picked up his scent and made her way right to his room on her own.

"If I hadn't seen it," said Elaine, "I wouldn't have believed it."

Now, Wendy, Richard, and Elaine are back at home, happily spending their days together. "She's just a part of us," said Elaine. "This is now a marriage of three."

WISE OWNERS
CANINE-LOVING CELEBS

Intelligence isn't just for the dogs! Our pups may be supersmart, but we humans are wise to have a dog (or two, or three!) around. Check out some of these famous celebrities sharing some love for our pooch pals.

PAUL MCCARTNEY
Musician

"We put a sound on 'Sergeant Pepper' only dogs can hear. If you ever play 'Sergeant Pepper,' watch your dog."

SIMON COWELL
Reality show host, on his dogs

"They've literally changed my life. I just love them."

THE OBAMAS

First Family of the United States

"Sasha and Malia, I love you more than you can imagine, and you have earned the new puppy that's coming with us to the White House."
—*Barack Obama in his 2008 presidential victory speech*

OPRAH WINFREY

Media mogul

"I am a woman who loves dogs. I've always loved dogs and I think that one of the reasons I love them so much is because as a child, I wasn't allowed to have them. As I grew up, the first thing I wanted was to get my own dog."

ELLEN DEGENERES

Talk show host

"I cannot imagine not going home to animals. They are the closest thing to God ... If I could, I would have 15 cats and 20 dogs."

BETTY WHITE

Actress

"Have you ever just taken a look at a golden retriever puppy? It's impossible to walk away!"

Border collie

Caring

LUCA

DEAF TO DISABILITY

Pit bull / New York

You don't necessarily have to hear the words "I love you" to know you are adored. Luca the deaf pit bull may not be able to hear it—but he knows his owners care.

When Luca was just a puppy, he was adopted and then returned to the ASPCA. The family that previously adopted him struggled to figure out how to train him since he couldn't hear their commands. But, when volunteer Dave Goldstein laid eyes on Luca at the shelter, it was love at first sight.

Dave's wife, Brooke Slater, came to the shelter to meet

Dalmatians have the highest percentage of inherited deafness of all dog breeds.

Luca and she too was smitten. They knew they wanted him to be part of their family, and they were most definitely up for the challenge of training a dog that couldn't hear their words.

From the start, they trained Luca to maintain eye contact with them so that he could see and follow their hand-signaled instructions. Some of the hand signals that Brooke and Dave use are similar to American Sign Language, and some are signs they invented. One example of a sign they use is thumb wiggling when they want to tell Luca, "Good boy." In total, Luca knows about eight to ten commands.

When Brooke smiles at him, Luca will wag his tail. Or, if he's done something naughty, she'll give him a "Mommy face" and he knows he's done something wrong and will lie down.

Brooke and Dave originally taught Luca to make eye contact because it was the only way they could communicate with him. But they quickly realized that making eye contact was a skill Luca could use in other situations. He now spends time with kids as a therapy dog, and he walks right up to them and looks them in the eyes. That sort of attention and connection seems to really make people happy.

Once, Luca visited a boy who had never taken a step without a walker. Luca kept watching him from across the room and wagging his tail. Then, for the first time, the boy stepped away from his walker, all on his own, just so that he could pet Luca.

Brooke and Dave have been so inspired by Luca that they started an organization called Bruised Not Broken, which helps rescue pit bulls and teach people about the breed.

After a day of working with kids, Luca is definitely tired. But as Brooke said, "The work he does, this is what he was born to do."

Pit Bull

ORIGIN: England

COLOR(S): Any color

HEIGHT: 17 to 19 inches (43 to 48 cm)

TEMPERAMENT: American Staffordshire terriers (aka pit bulls) are people-pleasing family dogs that flourish when given a job or activity.

COOPER

♥

NEVER LOSING SIGHT OF A BEST FRIEND

German shorthaired pointer / Kentucky

Cooper was born on the last day of grouse season, and for his owner, Mike Cole, a longtime Kentucky bird hunter, that meant this dog was sure to be special. Mike watched as Cooper was born, and it soon became clear that the two were a match made in hunting heaven.

Cooper is a German shorthaired pointer, one of the five oldest breeds of hunting dogs, and right away, he was a natural. He was still just a puppy, only four months old, and he was already helping Mike hunt by "pointing," which means he would aim his snout toward animals that he'd sniffed out.

Dogs can wiggle each nostril independently
to determine what direction
a smell is coming from.

Soon, Cooper learned to retrieve the grouse, pheasants, ducks, and quail that Mike shot. For two years, Cooper remained at Mike's side. They would travel together to different states to go hunting, and then at night, Cooper would sleep at the foot of Mike's bed. Many hunters and their bird dogs share a special bond, and Mike and Cooper became best friends.

One time, while out on a hunting trip, Cooper was sprayed in the face by a skunk. What began as a smelly nuisance may have ended up saving the pup's life. The next day as Mike was checking to make sure Cooper was okay, he noticed something wasn't quite right with his dog's eyes. At the vet, Mike learned Cooper had contracted an unrelated disease called blastomycosis, which is caused by a fungus, and can result in blindness.

Cooper had to have one of his eyes removed right away, and eventually became blind in the other. Even though it looked like the hunting career of his prodigy pup would be cut short, Mike was grateful that his buddy had survived. "Cooper the bird dog might be over," said Mike, "but Cooper my best friend will have a long life."

At first, Mike didn't know what the future would be like for Cooper. He wondered if it would be too dangerous for him to venture outside. But, thankfully, Cooper still tags along on all of Mike's hunting trips. He'll bump into things every once in a while, and the other dogs know to get out of his way when he comes bounding through the fields, but even though Cooper can no longer see, his hearing and sense of smell are tremendous. He happily runs around, following scent trails as well as Mike's voice.

Cooper is vibrant and active, and his heart is as big as ever. "I'd rather get one bird with him than five with my other dogs," said Mike. "It's not about the numbers but about quality time. It's about friends."

Cooper's special spirit has even inspired others who are enduring hardships. During one of the many vet visits after Cooper's diagnosis, Mike saw a young woman in the office who had just found out that her dog was going blind.

Mike thought meeting Cooper might cheer her up. So, he went to his truck and got Cooper, who hopped down without a leash and wagged his tail to greet them. When Mike told her that he was blind, she was surprised. He assured her that, even though it might be an adjustment, there were more happy times ahead. "You'll be closer than you've ever been," Mike told her. "You'll be his Seeing Eye Human."

ALFIE

♥

IN GOOD COMPANY

Labrador retriever mix / Ohio

Alfie, a yellow Labrador retriever mix, once tore a ligament in her knee and had to be taken to the emergency room. When she returned home, instead of one or two people waiting for her—like most dogs have—she had 20! Waiting on the front porch, to make sure their beloved pooch was okay, were the residents of the Victoria House, an assisted living facility in Austintown, Ohio.

The residents here enjoy a special, furry feature that sets the Victoria House apart from other facilities—Alfie, their very own dog.

One study found that interacting
with a dog might be helpful
to people suffering from dementia.

*No matter what the residents
and employees are up to, Alfie is
on hand to keep them company.*

Susan Greco, the activities director, thought of a way to brighten the lives of the elderly residents: Other facilities have dogs that come and visit, but wouldn't it be great if one could actually live with them, 24 hours a day!

Susan contacted Close to Home Animal Rescue, an organization that was just starting a program bringing dogs into nursing homes. They introduced her to three dogs, but Susan immediately fell for Alfie, an older dog who had been rescued from a shelter, where she would have been put down.

Alfie wasn't trained to be a therapy dog, but there was just something special about her. Right away she went up to three residents and let them pet her and cuddle her. It felt like "Miss Alfie," as the residents call her, belonged there.

At first, Alfie was a little nervous around the residents in wheelchairs. But Susan worked with Alfie until she became comfortable, and now she's perfectly at ease around them.

Alfie's nights are spent sleeping on a special bed under the nurses' station. Then each day, she walks around the facility, visiting the men and women and making them smile. She likes to go into the beauty salon and lie on the ground, to keep people company while they get their hair done.

Labrador Retriever

ORIGIN: Newfoundland, Canada

COLOR(S): Black, yellow, or chocolate brown

HEIGHT: 22 to 25 inches (56 to 64 cm)

TEMPERAMENT: Labrador retrievers are highly intelligent, gentle, and strong. They are wonderful family pets and are also often used as service dogs.

"People said we would have trouble getting people to take her out," said Susan. "But residents fight over walking her." It helps that Alfie has a very sweet, easygoing personality. She gets along well with kids that come to visit their grandparents and even other dogs that come by.

Alfie's situation is a win-win. She gets all sorts of attention, scratches, and cuddles, and in turn, she boosts the residents' spirits, encouraging them to be active. "We often say she was placed here for a reason," said Susan. "She has made a difference in all of our lives."

ASK AN **EXPERT**

Q: Why do humans love dogs so much?

Dr. Weitzman: As a species, dogs aren't threatening to humans, they're our companions. With dogs, there's no fear of them judging us. I'll get down on the floor and be totally sappy and sweet with my dogs, because I know they won't judge me. But with humans, I'm more reserved. And, dogs love us, too! A recent study found that dogs respond emotionally just like humans do. They have a great emotional capacity to love; that's not just in our heads.

The Snuggly Science of
Caring for Cuties

If you've ever felt stressed about homework and then searched for "cutest puppy ever" on the Internet, you're not alone. And, there's actually a scientific reason why it may have made you feel (and work!) better. Not only does looking at cute pictures of baby animals make you happy, a study in Japan found that it may also boost your attention to detail and overall work performance. Still not soothed? Well the only thing more fun than looking at a cute puppy is actually snuggling one. And scientifically speaking, it's good for you! When a person pets a dog, a hormone called oxytocin is released in the person's brain. This hormone is a chemical that helps lower our blood pressure and reduce stress. No wonder we feel so happy and calm after playing with our pups.

MR. GIBBS

♥

HELPING A LITTLE GIRL IN A BIG WAY

Goldendoodle / Georgia

When Alida Knobloch takes her turn on the slide, the next in line behind her isn't another five-year-old, it's her service dog, Mr. Gibbs. The loyal goldendoodle sits on the ground next to her while she swings in the backyard. When she rides in the cart at the grocery store, he's there too, walking beside it. He even has his own spot in the circle during story time at her preschool.

He is always by her side, which is exactly where he was trained to be, because Mr. Gibbs carries the oxygen tanks that Alida needs to help her breathe.

**Goldendoodles are a mix between
a golden retriever and a toy poodle.
They're known for being
very sweet, smart, and active.**

Alida was diagnosed with a disease called Neuroendocrine cell Hyperplasia of Infancy (NEHI) when she was just a baby. To keep her lungs and heart healthy, she needs to receive additional oxygen from portable oxygen tanks for all but one hour a day.

At first, her dad Aaron built rolling carts for her to carry her oxygen. But when she began walking, he and her mother, Debbie, wanted to figure out a way that Alida would be able to run, play, and be more independent.

One night, as Aaron and Debbie were watching TV, they saw a program on service animals. That's when Aaron had a life-changing idea. Instead of trying to build something that Alida would push in front of her, a better solution might be to find a way that Alida's oxygen would follow behind her. "The way to do that," said Aaron, "is with a service dog."

They researched their options and eventually decided to use a local dog trainer, Ashleigh Kinsley. When the Knoblochs called Ashleigh, she said she had just the dog for the job. When she introduced the family to Mr. Gibbs, he and Alida were fast friends.

Alida was just nearly three years old when she and Mr. Gibbs first started working together. Since Alida had just learned to talk, it took her some time to master the commands. But now they work very well together.

She gives commands like "Down," "Sit," and the most important one, "Let's go." Sometimes, like a typical little kid, she forgets to tell Mr. Gibbs

"The first time Ashleigh brought Mr. Gibbs over, he was seven or eight months old, and just this big, furry mess," Aaron said. "Alida played on the floor with him and laughed. We could tell that there was a connection there, and we suspected that this was going to work pretty well."

that they're going somewhere. But if she starts walking away, Mr. Gibbs will feel a little tug on his collar where the tube for her oxygen is attached, and that's a signal to him to follow her.

Mr. Gibbs takes his job very seriously and is very protective of Alida. He has even started to look out for her in ways he wasn't trained to. For example, he sleeps in a bed next to hers, and a couple of times at night he's let out a very distinct bark to get Aaron and Debbie's attention.

The first time he did it, they thought he needed to go outside. But when they brought him back up to Alida's room, he barked again. After they let him outside again and he barked a third time, they realized that Alida's oxygen had fallen out of her nose while she was sleeping, and Mr. Gibbs was trying to tell them. After Aaron fixed it, Mr. Gibbs jumped down and happily settled into his bed.

Mr. Gibbs does many important everyday tasks that make Alida's life easier. If Alida is having a hard day and isn't feeling well, Mr. Gibbs will lay right next to her and not leave her side. And even when she doesn't need Mr. Gibbs to carry her oxygen, if she gets up in the middle of the night to go to the bathroom, or if she needs to walk into a dark room, she brings him with her.

Mr. Gibbs and Alida share an incredible bond. And to Alida, Mr. Gibbs doesn't just help her carry around her oxygen or protect and look out for her—he's her best friend.

The Snuggly Science of
Caring for Cuties

Because we are wired to want to take care of our babies and protect them from danger, people are instinctively drawn to anything that resembles a human baby, even other animals that appear young, vulnerable, and harmless. Scientists have actually discovered certain physical traits that humans find cute, like bright eyes that sit low on a big round face, a pair of big round ears, floppy limbs and a side-to-side, teeter-tottering way of walking. Sound familiar? Um, puppies! We're so crazy for cute that we'll find ourselves fawning over baby bears, birds, and even bugs! If it's little, fuzzy, and has a sweet face, it doesn't matter what species it is, we're bound to think it's cute. Awww!

CARING BUDDIES
ODD DOG FRIENDSHIPS

We're not the only ones crazy for dogs. Check out these adorable pups and the surprising animals who love them.

Who: Bella & Tarra

What: Dog and Elephant

How They Show They Care: Bella rolls onto her back and lets Tarra pet her belly with her trunk. The two go on walks together and sleep side by side. Once when Bella got hurt, Tarra waited outside the vet's office every day while she healed.

Who: Earl & Fred

What: Dog and Potbellied Pig

How They Show They Care: If the two pals run into another dog, Earl, a Great Dane, will stand in front of Fred to protect him from harm. They sleep in the same room, and when Fred goes outside to graze in the grass, Earl goes right along with him.

Who: Cleo & Sterling

What: Dog and Duck

How They Show They Care: At first Cleo didn't want to be friends, but Sterling, the determined duck, followed him everywhere he went. Now they play in the pond together, explore the tall grass in the backyard, share meals, and even sleep in the same kennel.

Who: Maddy & Finnegan

What: Dog and Squirrel

How They Show They Care: Maddy was just about to give birth to a litter of puppies when her owner rescued the three-day-old squirrel. Maddy pulled Finnegan in with her new babies, licked him, fed him, and raised him just like one of her own.

Who: Augie & Suzy

What: Dog and Chimpanzee

How They Show They Care: When Suzy's mother passed away, Augie stepped in to help care for her. Suzy climbs on Augie like a jungle gym, rides on his back, and feeds the pooch jelly sandwiches after he's eaten all his food. If Suzy ever gets scared, she runs right to Augie, her best friend.

Mixed breed

Strong

RICOCHET

♥

RIDING THE WAVES TO HELP KIDS IN NEED

Golden retriever / California

 Ricochet is a pooch that loves to hop on her surfboard to enjoy the salty splash of the ocean, the warm sun shining on a clear day, and a quick doggie paddle in the water. Ricochet loves to ride the waves—as a dog surfer!

From the time she was born, Ricochet was trained to be a service dog. And for the first four months of her life, the sweet-natured golden retriever was a model student, doing exactly as told. When given the command, she would obediently open the fridge or turn off the lights.

> Dogs have webbing between their toes—
> **kind of like a duck!**—which makes them
> natural swimmers.

But eventually, something changed. She no longer wanted to follow commands, and would walk away or just lie down instead. Her owner, Judy Fridono, began to worry. She took Ricochet to doctors and trainers, but nothing seemed to work.

Little did Judy know, Ricochet was an extraordinary dog that was going to inspire people all over the world, she just had other ideas about how she was going to serve.

And although Ricochet wasn't interested in much of the service dog training, there was one part that Ricochet did seem to like. It was an activity used to develop coordination in which the dogs would balance on a surfboard in a kiddie pool.

When Judy heard there was a surfing competition for dogs near their home in California, she decided to give it a try. She figured Ricochet would ride a few waves and that would be it. But much to her surprise, Ricochet

SWEAT PANTS

Unlike humans, who have sweat glands all over their bodies, dogs' sweat glands are in the pads of their feet. That's why if your dog just came in from outside on a hot day, you may notice a trail of wet paw prints through the house. Sweating is the body's way of cooling off, and since dogs have far fewer sweat glands than we do, they need another way to lower their body temperature. So, they pant. By opening their mouth and sticking out their tongue, it allows the water to evaporate. Then, their heavy breathing gets air circulating throughout their body. This is one reason why it's not safe to use muzzles that prohibit dogs from panting.

Patrick Ivison and Ricochet catch a wave while others cheer them on.

ended up winning third place. "I was brought to tears," she said. "It was the first time after all those months she was really good at something."

Judy realized that Ricochet had a very unique skill, and she wanted to figure out a way it could be used to help people. She reached out to Patrick Ivison, a high school student who was paralyzed in an accident as a baby. Together they planned an event in which Patrick and Ricochet would surf side by side on separate boards to raise money for Patrick's physical therapy.

But, once again, Ricochet had a different plan.

On one of the first rides, she jumped off her board and onto Patrick's. It worked well and Patrick was happy to ride together. So, they got a bigger board, put Ricochet on the back, and then pushed the two of them into a wave. "It worked perfectly," said Patrick.

The event raised $10,000 and also helped Patrick earn a grant to pay for three years of his physical therapy. Since then, Ricochet has helped raise more than 30 times that amount by surfing alone or with someone with a physical impairment.

As a dog, Ricochet is able to help balance the board when the human surfer might not be able to. She instinctively knows where she should stand on the board in order to adjust to the person's disability. She'll stand at the front, at the back, or even sideways in order to maintain balance.

Patrick has received emails from people all over the world who have seen videos of them online, saying that he and Ricochet have inspired them to keep fighting and to have hope. "Ricochet was supposed to be a service dog," said Patrick. "But instead of serving just one family, she has gotten to help millions."

Judy agrees. She said, "Ricochet took a different journey than I thought she would, but looking back on it, it all makes perfect sense. None of this would have happened if I hadn't let her be who she needed to be."

Dog-abunga, dude!

HOOCH

♥

THE ULTIMATE ADRENALINE DOGGIE

Mixed breed / Australia

 Sean Herbert was getting on a plane to go skydiving when his little dog, Hooch, scampered after him on the tarmac. Someone holding the plane door picked her up and said to Sean, "Is this yours?" The plane was about to leave, and Sean knew the pilot couldn't look after a puppy on the plane once everyone had jumped, so he made a game-time decision: He duct-taped her to the inside of his suit.

"She seemed pretty happy," said Sean. The two made their first tandem jump that day and began what would become a lifetime of adventure for Hooch.

One man and his dog set a world record for highest man-dog parachute deployment. The pup was strapped into a harness designed for war dogs deployed on aerial missions.

Hooch seemed to enjoy skydiving so much that eventually Sean had a special skydiving suit designed for her. Once a week, Hooch would get strapped to Sean and the two would jump out of a plane with a parachute.

Sean adopted Hooch, a mix of Cavalier King Charles spaniel and blue heeler, from a pound in Australia. The two instantly bonded and remained inseparable. Since Sean loves adventure sports, Hooch always tagged along.

Hooch loved being Sean's co-captain and sometimes rode with him on his motorcycle and Jet Ski. When Sean first brought Hooch scuba diving, Hooch jumped overboard and attempted to dive after him. Since Hooch enjoyed the water and seemed willing to dive, Sean designed a special suit so that she could scuba dive too!

Sean worked with engineers to create custom equipment for Hooch. First, they needed to attach a tiny mask to an oxygen tank. Then, a wet suit company made her a special outfit. After practicing in a pool, they moved on

Hooch made 14 scuba dives and 53 parachute jumps with her owner Sean.

to shallow parts of the ocean. Eventually, Sean and his fearless furry friend went scuba diving on coral reefs.

Hooch was so comfortable diving that when they would reach the ocean floor, she would walk away from Sean to explore the underwater world. "She was very interested in what was going on," said Sean.

Hooch went scuba diving 14 times and skydiving 53 times in her lifetime. She eventually was forced to retire after she broke her leg falling from a bed. She passed away when she was 15 years old, due to a genetic defect that is common in King Charles spaniels. But there's no doubt that Hooch was an exceptional dog that led a life chock-full of incredible, fun adventures.

PICASSO

 George Gallego was paralyzed from the waist down in an accident more than 20 years ago. But despite his physical limitations, today he's a world-class athlete and participates in triathlons around the globe. He's even enlisted a special running partner to help him train for his races—his pit bull, Picasso. This strong pup is built to work out!

George rescued Picasso when Picasso was just six weeks old. Right away the pup began training to become a therapy and service dog so that he could help George with tasks like

Some dogs can really run far!
Sled dogs in the Iditarod race run about
1,000 miles (1,609 km) over the course of 9 to
15 days through the Alaskan wilderness.

opening and closing doors and picking things up off the floor. Then, George's wife, who is a marathon runner, began training Picasso to run alongside George's hand-operated cycle called a push-rim racing chair.

As an athlete competing in long-distance events, it's important to keep a steady pace so that you don't run out of steam too quickly. That's where Picasso comes in. As a dog, he naturally keeps a steady pace, so if George sticks with him, it helps him maintain a consistent speed.

Running with Picasso also has the added bonus of having a built-in running buddy. "He keeps me company when I am doing four- to six-hour training runs," said George.

And, if George ever needs a little help, Picasso is right there. Once, George hurt his shoulder and was having trouble pushing uphill. Picasso stepped in and pulled him the rest of the way, up and over the hill.

Following his accident, George had a tough time adjusting to his physical limitations. But then, he decided to make some changes, get in shape, and soon he was preparing for his first road race. The challenge of competing in the races, and the sense of accomplishment, made him feel empowered.

George founded an organization called Wheels of Progress, which aims to provide housing for people with physical disabilities. As time went on, George began participating in more and more races to raise money and awareness for the cause.

In 2011, George completed the New York City triathlon, which included a 1-mile (1.6-km) swim, a 25-mile (40-km) ride on a hand-propelled bicycle, and a 7-mile (11-km) road race in a push-rim racing chair. Thanks to his fundraising for the event, he was able to help a 21-year-old with a spinal cord injury move out of a nursing home intended for seniors and into an apartment. And after the race, Picasso was waiting—with tail wagging—in the VIP tent to greet him.

It's not just when training for races that Picasso empowers his owner. George says that if he ever feels down after a long, hard day, Picasso is there to lift his spirits. "One look into his eyes and my worries are gone," he said.

"I never understood the phrase 'A dog is a man's best friend' until he entered my life," said George. "He is so loyal and willing to please, how can a dog not be a man's best friend?"

TILLMAN

♥

FORGET FETCH — LET'S SKATEBOARD!

English bulldog / California

When Tillman was just a puppy, he discovered his favorite toy. But unlike some dogs, it wasn't a tennis ball or even a Frisbee—it was a skateboard!

Tillman had been watching his older brother, a Rottweiler named Stoli, play with the skateboard and Tillman wanted in on the action. His owner, Ron Davis, could see how badly Tillman wanted to try skateboarding, but since Tillman is an English bulldog and has little legs, a regular-size skateboard was too big for him. So, Ron decided to make one special for him.

Tillman loved his new board! From the time he woke up to the time he went to bed, all he wanted to do was play with it. As soon as Tillman was big enough, Ron started teaching him how to balance on the board.

By the time Tillman was eight months old, he could stand with two legs on the skateboard and push with the other two on the ground. He could also stand with all four legs on top of the board. Tillman was quickly becoming a neighborhood celebrity. It's not every day you see a skateboarding dog!

Ron posted a video of Tillman skateboarding on YouTube, and right away, people from all over the world started calling, wanting to hear more about him. Tillman has traveled all over North America to skate in front of audiences. He's even starred in a TV show! Today, Tillman is eight years old, and not only does he still love to skateboard, he also snowboards, wakeboards, and surfs. "He loves a challenge," said Ron.

Even though he rides all the time, when he sees his skateboard, he gets

Tillman is one athletic pooch. He also loves snowboarding and surfing!

CHEW ON THIS

All domesticated dogs are descendants of wolves, and just like wolves, dogs have 42 teeth. Four of those 42 are long, sharp canine teeth, or fangs (two on the top, two on the bottom). These teeth are made for catching and tearing food, as well as fighting predators. Even though domesticated dogs no longer hunt for their food, the urge to chew is still very strong. That's why, when left alone, dogs will chew on furniture. It's also why dogs love chew toys so much! And, when a dog feels threatened and pulls back their lips to reveal their teeth, it's their way of showing aggressors their greatest weapon and letting them know to stay back.

just as excited as he did when he was a puppy. He starts barking like crazy and jumping up and down—he just can't wait to get on that board.

The one thing he hasn't quite mastered yet is stopping. So instead, to avoid running into things, he turns by shifting his weight to the left or right. He can even flip the board and ride up and down ramps. "He's like a person now," said Ron.

Tillman even has a little ritual he performs before he hops on the board. Just like a basketball player who always dribbles the ball three times before shooting a foul shot, Tillman chews all four of the wheels for about a minute before he rides.

Tillman loves riding so much that if Ron let him, he would skate all day. "Once, I put out a hamburger and the skateboard," said Ron. "Tillman went right to the skateboard." Tillman, it seems, has eyes for only one thing!

English Bulldog

ORIGIN: England

COLOR(S): Brown and white, black and white, white, red, or various shades of brown.

HEIGHT: 12 to 15 inches (30 to 38 cm)

TEMPERAMENT: Sweet, loyal, and need minimal grooming and exercise. Often snore and are prone to overheating, so provide lots of rest breaks!

PUDSEY

♥

DANCING TO STARDOM
Mixed breed / United Kingdom

 In 2012, two amazing dancers were named the winners of *Britain's Got Talent*. They had spent the whole season jumping and jiving around a stage together in front of thousands of adoring fans. Even the notoriously crabby judge, Simon Cowell, was smitten with the pair. Ashleigh Butler hugged her partner and buried her face into his neck. And then …

He wagged his furry little tail.

Pudsey was the first dog to ever win *Britain's Got Talent* and his owner, Ashleigh, couldn't have been more proud. Six years earlier, on her 11th birthday, Ashleigh opened a huge present and found a little squirming puppy inside. It was the adorable, fluffy Pudsey, a cross between a border collie, bichon frise and Chinese crested.

Ashleigh, who trained her first dog when she was just five years old, started training Pudsey right away. Ashleigh's mom trained dogs, and she grew up training them as well. Up to that point, Ashleigh had mainly trained dogs in agility, teaching them how to complete various obstacles. But as soon as she saw canine freestyling performed—when a dog performs tricks and creative moves to music—Ashleigh wanted to try it.

One of the things that makes Ashleigh and Pudsey unique is that Ashleigh dances with him. Their performances are very lively and fast paced and usually have themes like *The Flintstones* and *Mission: Impossible.* Some of Pudsey's most well-known moves are when he jumps onto Ashleigh's back, jumps through her arms (which she makes into the shape of a hoop), and walks on his hind legs.

Pudsey and Ashleigh pose after their big win on Britain's Got Talent.

ASK AN **EXPERT**

Q: Why can some dogs do amazing things?

Dr. Weitzman: There are more than 330 official breeds of dogs, and humans created those breeds to achieve different functions. Depending on the breed, we domesticated them to have different proportions of various skills. Some are very athletic, some are exceptionally strong, some are good at retrieving things, and others are smart enough to be taught to perform specific tasks.

FUR COAT

A dog's coat is pretty amazing. Aside from being soft to pet, it serves a serious function. You may have seen a big, fluffy dog walking on a hot day and thought, *That poor dog, it must be so hot!* But dogs' coats act just like insulation on a home; they keep them warm in the winter and cool in the summer. So, don't be too quick to shave your dog in the warmer months. Without their coat to help cool them down, they may be more prone to overheating. Also, their hair protects their sensitive skin from getting sunburned.

"He walks so straight and upright," said Ashleigh. "He actually walks like a little human." Pudsey enjoys doing this particular move so much that once he's up on his hind legs, Ashleigh sometimes has trouble getting him to come back down onto all fours.

Some dogs might get scared of all of the hooting and hollering, but Pudsey loves the energy and excitement of a live crowd. "I encourage the audience to cheer for him," said Ashleigh. "He loves it! He's a bit of a show-off."

Sometimes Pudsey gets so carried away during a performance that he'll stop doing the routine they've rehearsed and start doing some of his own moves. Ashleigh will then quickly improvise to make it look like it was all part of the plan. "The audience seems to prefer what he does," she said. "So he's obviously doing something right."

Since winning *Britain's Got Talent,* Ashleigh and Pudsey have become stars in England. They met the Queen of England, flew on Simon Cowell's private jet to the United States, and Pudsey even starred in a movie, *Pudsey: The Movie.* "Pudsey did everything himself in the movie," said Ashleigh. "Even all the stunts, which were his favorite part."

It's so much fun to watch this dancing duo because it's clear that they're crazy about each other and they're having fun. Pudsey loves to train, but even more than that, he loves to put on a show. "Getting to perform in front of other people, while doing something he loves," said Ashleigh, "it just makes him extra happy."

SUPER-STRONG PUPS

EXTREME BREEDS

All dogs are awesome, but some breeds have certain physical advantages that give them superspecial skills. Check out some of these dogs bred for their amazing talents!

Breed: Bloodhound

Special Skill: Tracking

How They Do It: They have such a strong sense of smell that they can detect something that was there days before the dog arrived. Their long, floppy ears help them hold and find scents, too.

Breed: St. Bernard

Special Skill: Mountain Rescues

How They Do It: Their large bodies give them strength and stamina, and their huge feet are ideal for trekking through the snow.

Breed: Newfoundland
Special Skill: Swimming
How They Do It: Their dense coats protect them from icy water. Plus they have webbed feet.

Breed: Fox Terrier
Special Skill: Digging
How They Do It: Their shoulders and front legs are angled in just the right position for digging, and their small size is perfect for wriggling down burrows.

Breed: Greyhound
Special Skill: Running
How They Do It: A greyhound's sleek streamlined body means less wind resistance for faster speed. Its long legs and lung capacity also give it an edge.

Breed: Siberian Husky
Special Skill: Pulling
How They Do It: Well-developed chest muscles help them pull sleds through the snow. Thick coats keep them warm in chilly weather.

FAITH

♥

DEFYING THE ODDS
Mixed breed / Indiana

Faith was found at a flea market in Indiana when she was just three weeks old. She was missing one of her front legs and was unable to use the other. When Jude Stringfellow's son brought Faith home, Jude worried that the young puppy might not survive.

Jude tried to prepare her three kids for what might happen, and she explained that Faith might not live through the night. Jude and her family decided they would try to make her as comfortable as they could.

Faith, however, had her own plans.

A true fighter, Faith survived the night and began to thrive throughout the following weeks. At first, she could only move around by scooting. She would push with her back legs and slide her upper body on the ground. The vet warned that eventually the rubbing would injure Faith's chest and chin, so Jude and her family began training her to lift her head by holding a spoonful of peanut butter above her.

When Faith was six weeks old, they set her down outside in snow. When she felt the cold on her belly, she popped right up and sat on her haunches. The Stringfellows were ecstatic and showered her with praise and treats. Now that she was up, they encouraged her to hop forward by calling her name and offering her a treat. And, just like a kangaroo, she did. It was amazing!

When Faith was three months old, one of the other dogs in the house began teasing and nipping at her. Faith was fed up, so she stood on her two back legs, just like a person, and took off running.

Jude realized how special Faith was and how happy it would make other people to see her walk. She began taking Faith to nursing homes, hospitals, and eventually to visit wounded veterans. Faith's resilience and persistence inspired others who had been injured. She gave people hope and made them smile.

Faith has traveled to military bases all around the United States and beyond. Faith has even been made an honorary sergeant in the U.S. Army for her work. Sometimes having Faith around makes it easier for veterans to open up about their own experiences.

"Sometimes she just sits and listens," said Jude, "and sometimes she crawls into their lap."

Faith has inspired many, many people to keep trying and to push past their limitations. Jude now gives motivational speeches and even wrote about her powerful pup in the book, *Faith Walks* (some of the money from each sale goes to charity).

As Jude said, "Faith is what it looks like to be positive and persevere."

Jude's daughter, Laura, plays with Faith (far right) and another family dog.

IZZY

♥

THE POWER OF FRIENDSHIP

Black-and-tan coonhound / Florida

 Izzy, a sweet, floppy-eared coonhound, came into Gabrielle Ford's life when she needed a friend the most. Gabrielle has a rare neuromuscular disease called Friedreich's ataxia, which made walking difficult by the time she entered high school.

For years, bullies at Gabrielle's school tormented her because of her condition. Then, at her graduation ceremony, as she walked across the stage to accept her diploma, she fell. Afraid the bullying would continue, Gabrielle no longer wanted to leave her house.

Early American hunters bred coonhounds to find "tree raccoons." The dogs can follow a raccoon's scent even after it climbs a tree, and they make sure it stays there until the hunters arrive.

Over the next few years, Gabrielle's condition progressed and soon she needed a wheelchair. She went out less and less. The less she socialized, the more depressed and lonely she became.

But then, something happened that changed her life. She adopted her precious puppy, Izzy.

From the moment her parents said she could have a dog, things starting look up. Just preparing for Izzy's arrival began to lift Gabrielle's spirits. She even started leaving the house more to buy Izzy food and toys. "I could feel myself coming out of my shell," said Gabrielle.

When Izzy finally arrived, Gabrielle instantly felt her happiness and bravery returning. "I felt so comfortable with her," she said. "I could talk to her about anything and she was my best friend."

When Izzy was a little less than three years old, she too was diagnosed with a rare muscular disease. The symptoms were similar to the ones Gabrielle experienced and just like her owner, Izzy was feeling extremely tired and was very unsteady on her feet. "I was devastated," said Gabrielle. But going through it together bonded the two even more.

Animal Planet heard about Izzy and Gabrielle's close friendship and how similar their conditions were, and featured them on an episode. After it aired, people from all over wrote in to say how inspired they were by their story.

Then, Gabrielle began receiving requests to visit schools to talk about her experiences with bullying. Izzy's comforting presence gave Gabrielle the courage to face her fears and help others.

"I was absolutely panicked, and there was no way I could have done it without Izzy," said Gabrielle. But when they walked into a room together, people weren't looking at Gabrielle or her wheelchair, all eyes were on Izzy. "Everyone just loved her," she said.

For eight years, the two traveled to schools around the country giving presentations about bullying and its terrible effects. Izzy lived until she was almost ten years old, and Gabrielle continues to speak in her honor. Izzy was a shining light in Gabrielle's life. "She changed me," said Gabrielle. "If it wasn't for her, I would still be a fearful person hiding away in my house."

Even though she no longer stands by Gabrielle's side, Izzy will live forever in her heart.

JASMINE

♥

A MOTHER TO MANY

Greyhound / England

When police officers in England found Jasmine, she was malnourished and had been locked in a shed. She was dirty and hungry, and it was clear she had been abused. Little did they know then that this golden greyhound had a heart of gold.

The police brought her to the Nuneaton and Warwickshire Wildlife Sanctuary, where the founder, Geoff Grewcock, and his staff showered Jasmine with love and affection. Within a month, she was beginning to feel better and became more trusting of humans.

Though greyhounds are speed machines and can run up to 43 miles per hour (69 kph), they're actually very calm and quiet indoors, and they love to lie around and relax.

"You could tell that she was a very gentle dog by nature," said Geoff.

Then, the most beautiful thing happened: Jasmine began taking care of other animals at the shelter, just as she would her own puppies.

She first set her sights on Toby and Buster, a pair of abandoned puppies. Upon their arrival, Jasmine approached the puppies and began licking them. Just like a mother would, she'd pick them up in her mouth to carry them around the sanctuary.

Next, she met Roxy, a three-month-old fox that had been found tied to a railing. Roxy would cry and whine when she was left alone, so Jasmine would comfort and lick her, or just lie down beside her. "And Roxy would stop, immediately," said Geoff.

Jasmine went on to nurture many animals in this way. In fact, she helped take care of Bramble, an 11-week-old baby deer, or fawn; Cleo, a Canada goose; 5 fox cubs; 4 badger cubs; 8 guinea pigs; and 15 rabbits. "There are

This greyhound's love knew no bounds. Jasmine (far right) is pictured with some of her other animal friends.

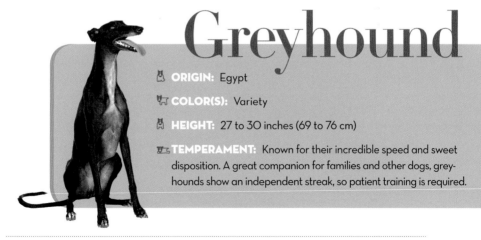

Greyhound

ORIGIN: Egypt

COLOR(S): Variety

HEIGHT: 27 to 30 inches (69 to 76 cm)

TEMPERAMENT: Known for their incredible speed and sweet disposition. A great companion for families and other dogs, greyhounds show an independent streak, so patient training is required.

Q: Why do dogs bring out the best in us?

Dr. Weitzman: I've noticed that dogs take us out of ourselves. If you've had a bad day and then you see your dog, they're not concerned with the details. They center you by snapping you out of the stress whirlwind. Also, dogs and cats are some of the only creatures in the animal world that we have such an intimate relationship with. They remind us that we're not the only ones on the planet. That's part of why they're so inspiring to us. Even people who don't relate to other humans, melt over dogs and cats. Even grumpy people love dogs! Why? Because dogs let them.

certain things only an animal mother can provide, and Jasmine provided it," said Geoff.

Jasmine's instinct to nuzzle and lick the baby animals, like foxes, badgers, and squirrels, actually served a greater purpose. As Geoff explained, "They need a warm lick on their bellies to stimulate feeding and urinating."

Then there was Parsley, another greyhound at the sanctuary who had to wear a muzzle before he met Jasmine. Jasmine's friendship calmed him until his aggression ceased and the muzzle was removed.

Geoff eventually adopted Jasmine as his personal pet. Her generous and warm heart inspired everyone who knew her. "She loved meeting new people," he said. "She would always come running out of the house to give them a friendly lick."

Jasmine passed away in 2011, but her memory lives on. People in the town came to a service for the beloved dog, and then Geoff and his coworkers began receiving letters and emails from people around the world who wanted to pay their respects to Jasmine. People even sent donations to help keep the sanctuary running.

In a special way, Jasmine continued to take care of the sanctuary and its animals even after she was gone.

INSPIRING
Words About Dogs

Happiness is a warm puppy.

— Charles M. Schulz

Charles M. Schulz was an American cartoonist who created the comic "Peanuts," which features Charlie Brown and his beagle, Snoopy. The first drawing Schulz had ever published was a picture of his family dog, Spike, in the newspaper feature "Ripley's Believe It or Not."

IDGIE & RUTH

♥

A CAT'S BEST FRIEND

Dachshund and cat / Florida

When an animal control officer found Idgie and Ruth, they were sitting at the end of a stranger's driveway in rural Florida. Idgie, a dachshund, was covered in ants. But even that couldn't keep her from the one thing she'd made her mission: protecting her best friend, Ruth, a disabled cat.

When the officer finally got past Ruth's barking bodyguard, he saw right away that Ruth didn't have full use of her legs and wasn't able to stand. At first, the animal control facility separated Idgie and Ruth.

But it wasn't long before Idgie cried and howled until the workers realized that these two were much happier when they were together.

When no one came to claim them, animal control called Jackie Borum, who runs Hollywood Houndz Boutique and Spa. At the store, they board and groom animals, but they also foster rescue animals and put them up for adoption. When Jackie met Idgie and Ruth, right away she could see they were very special. "Idgie is so loyal and committed to Ruth," said Jackie. "They have a very special friendship."

Jackie had rescued Idgie and Ruth with the intention of finding them another home, but soon Jackie decided to adopt them herself. She wanted to make sure this special pair was kept together. After many visits to many doctors, they still haven't been able to figure out the cause of Ruth's disability. But for now, Ruth isn't letting it slow her down. Ruth is able to scoot and climb and she loves playing with string. She's a determined, feisty kitty and even though she can't walk, she finds ways to get around.

Ruth and Idgie spend their days with Jackie and her co-workers at the store, where they've made lots of new friends. There are four shop cats, one bunny named Cadbury, a dog named Poky, and up to 40 other animals at any time.

Idgie and Ruth share a space near the front of the store, where they love looking out the window. But when new dogs come into the store, Idgie gets very protective of Ruth and will stand guard in front of her so that no other animals can get close. The two friends like to snuggle and play, and whenever Idgie gets a new toy, she takes it over to Ruth so that they can share.

"They have such a special bond," said Jackie. "I think anyone would be lucky to have a friend like Idgie."

INSPIRING
Words About Dogs

There's nothing—nothing—on the face of this beautiful earth, as wonderful as a puppy.

— Ree Drummond

Ree Drummond is the star of the Food Network show *The Pioneer Woman*, and author of the children's book series *Charlie the Ranch Dog*, which she wrote about her beloved basset hound, Charlie.

KUCHAR

♥

A VETERAN'S SECOND CHANCE
English Labrador / Alabama

 Sometimes, dogs give us that little spark we need when we're down and out. And that's exactly what one special pup did for a war veteran who desperately needed some inspiration and love to raise his spirits.

When Spc. Karl Fleming returned from serving in Afghanistan in 2011, he was suffering from nerve damage to his back, leg, and shoulder, as well as from a traumatic brain injury. Karl had a lot of anxiety, and everyday activities like going to the grocery store or eating at a restaurant became too difficult for him.

According to the Americans with Disabilities Act, all registered service dogs are allowed to accompany their owners wherever members of the public are allowed.

He had nightmares, he would sleep late into the day, and he stopped wanting to hang out with other people.

Karl knew someone who had a service dog through the organization K9s for Warriors, and after talking to his doctors, he contacted them about adopting a dog of his own. That's when he met Kuchar, a beautiful, cream-colored English Labrador.

Kuchar is one of many dogs trained by K9s for Warriors to help veterans. The dogs are rescued from shelters and trained to perform tasks that help with the specific sorts of issues affecting soldiers.

Karl and Kuchar were matched based on Karl's needs and Kuchar's strengths. Right away, Kuchar began having a positive impact on Karl's life. Instead of sleeping late, Karl needed to get up to feed Kuchar and take her outside.

Karl would regularly take her out for walks, and little by little he felt more confident to try things that once made him uncomfortable.

Kuchar goes everywhere with Karl and is able to sense when he starts feeling anxious. When that happens, Kuchar will sit on Karl's feet to let him know she's there, or even jump up in his lap to comfort him and help him feel safe. "She's something else," said Karl. "She's so sweet."

Kuchar wears a vest when she and Karl leave the house to let people know that she's a service dog. When the vest is on, she's on duty and she takes that very seriously. But then, when they get home and the vest comes off, she's ready to have fun. She loves to play and be goofy. "She's very boisterous and outgoing," said Karl. "We call her the wrecking ball because when she comes in a room, it's all about her."

At night, Kuchar sleeps against Karl. And if he begins to show signs that he's having a nightmare, by tossing and turning or seeming distressed, Kuchar lays across his chest. If Karl begins having night sweats, Kuchar will even lick his face.

For many soldiers who are return-ing from war, it's unnerving to have

As a service dog, Kuchar is trained to respond to Karl's specific needs.

Another thing Karl loves about Kuchar? Her animated eyes and black jowls make it look like she's always smiling.

someone walk up behind them and surprise them. To make sure that doesn't happen, Kuchar lays down behind Karl when they're in line at places like the grocery store. When Karl moves closer to the register, Kuchar stands up, takes a few steps forward and then lays down again to protect her owner.

Soldiers in the army are taught to have a battle buddy. They're someone who looks out for your safety and well-being. "They'll say, 'Battle buddy's got your 6,' which means they have your back and they're looking behind you," said Karl. "That's what Kuchar does. She is a battle buddy to me."

INSPIRING
Words About Dogs

Marley

Dogs are great. Bad dogs, if you can really call them that, are perhaps the greatest of them all. — John Grogan

John Grogan is the author of *Marley and Me*, the best-selling book about a family and their lovable, but superspunky (and a bit naughty) dog, Marley. The book was made into a hit movie with Jennifer Aniston and Owen Wilson.

INSPIRED BY STARDOM

WELCOME TO HOLLYWOOF

Mathilde de Cagny has trained furry, four-legged stars for many films, including *Hotel for Dogs*, *Marley and Me*, *Hugo*, and *We Bought a Zoo*. Here she talks about how she got started, some of her favorite projects, and what it is she loves about her job.

Q: **How did you get started training animals?**

A: I was born with a love of animals and I was always very curious about animal psychology. One day, I saw a cat food commercial where the cat had to jump up on the table and knock down the bag in order to get to his food. I realized then that training animals was

Havanese

indeed a job. And, from then on, I was obsessed with it. I thought, *This is what I'm going to do—I'm going to train animals for motion pictures and TV!* So, I watched a bunch of movies with animals, wrote down the trainers' names and then I contacted them and volunteered for their companies. I got really lucky because my first dog was one that I found in a shelter and he was chosen for the movies *Back to the Future 2* and *3*.

Q: **What do you look for in a dog that you're going to train?**

A: Well, 80 percent of my dogs are rescues, so the goal is to pick up dogs in need and give them a second chance. For example, I trained the dog in *Anchorman 1* and *2,* and he was actually found in a parking lot in Virginia. It doesn't have to be the most beautiful dog, but there has to be something about him that's going to make me look twice—maybe some funny ears or a tongue hanging out. I like them when they're not perfect. As for their demeanor, I like dogs that are really hyper and outgoing. I like dogs that may have too much energy for a family, because there is never too much energy for the type of work that we do.

Q: **Can you give an example of a particularly difficult scene or trick?**

A: I have to be honest with you, usually when I read a script, I think, I'll never be able to do it! But training is a process and when you take your time and try out different approaches, ultimately you get to where you need to go. In *Hugo,* there's a scene where the dog is in a clock tower and he's looking for the main character. It was shot in such a way that I couldn't be anywhere close to the dog. So, I taught her how to search for treats. Then, I hid radios in the clock tower and I called her from downstairs, through the radios. That way, I was able to get her moving around the tower. It looked great!

Q: **Do you have any tips for someone who might want to train their own dog?**

A: I want to emphasize that I train with positive reinforcement and I always make sure it feels like a fun game for the dog. The clicker is a great tool to use and training is a great way to bond with your dog.

Q: **What is your favorite part of what you do?**

A: I love so many things, but I love the animals more than anything. To be able to spend my days with them is such a blessing.

The Final Woof

Cocker spaniel

"Dogs are not our whole life,
but they make our lives whole."

—Roger Caras,
animal welfare advocate

Credits

From the Publisher: All stories, except Lucy; Mama, Jake, Mishka, and Stryder; Angel; Charlie Boy; Mr. Gibbs; Tillman; Pudsey; Idgie and Ruth; and Kuchar have been adapted from the National Geographic book *Devoted: 38 Extraordinary Tales of Love, Loyalty, and Life With Dogs* by Rebecca Ascher-Walsh.

STAFF FOR THIS BOOK

Kate Olesin, *Project Editor*
James Hiscott Jr., *Art Director & Design*
Hillary Leo, *Photo Editor*
Ruthie Thompson, *Designer*
Paige Towler, *Editorial Assistant*
Sanjida Rashid, *Design Production Assistant*
Michael Libonati, *Special Projects Assistant*
Grace Hill, *Associate Managing Editor*
Joan Gossett, *Production Editor*
Lewis R. Bassford, *Production Manager*
George Bounelis, *Manager, Production Services*
Susan Borke, *Legal and Business Affairs*

PUBLISHED BY THE NATIONAL GEOGRAPHIC SOCIETY

Gary E. Knell, *President and CEO*
John M. Fahey, *Chairman of the Board*
Melina Gerosa Bellows, *Chief Education Officer*
Declan Moore, *Chief Media Officer*
Hector Sierra, *Senior Vice President and General Manager, Book Division*

SENIOR MANAGEMENT TEAM, KIDS PUBLISHING & MEDIA

Nancy Laties Feresten, *Senior Vice President;* Jennifer Emmett, *Vice President, Editorial Director, Kids Books;* Julie Vosburgh Agnone, *Vice President, Editorial Operations;* Rachel Buchholz, *Editor and Vice President, NG Kids magazine;* Michelle Sullivan, *Vice President, Kids Digital;* Eva Absher-Schantz, *Design Director;* Jay Sumner, *Photo Director;* Hannah August, *Marketing Director;* R. Gary Colbert, *Production Director*

DIGITAL

Anne McCormack, *Director;* Laura Goertzel, Sara Zeglin, *Producers;* Jed Winer, *Special Projects Assistant;* Emma Rigney, *Creative Producer;* Brian Ford, *Video Producer;* Bianca Bowman, *Assistant Producer;* Natalie Jones, *Senior Product Manager*

The National Geographic Society is one of the world's largest nonprofit scientific and educational organizations. Founded in 1888 to "increase and diffuse geographic knowledge," the Society's mission is to inspire people to care about the planet. It reaches more than 400 million people worldwide each month through its official journal, *National Geographic,* and other magazines; National Geographic Channel; television documentaries; music; radio; films; books; DVDs; maps; exhibitions; live events; school publishing programs; interactive media; and merchandise. National Geographic has funded more than 10,000 scientific research, conservation, and exploration projects and supports an education program promoting geographic literacy.

For more information, please visit nationalgeographic.com, call 1-800-NGS LINE (647-5463), or write to the following address:

National Geographic Society
1145 17th Street N.W.
Washington, D.C. 20036-4688 U.S.A.

Visit us online at nationalgeographic.com/books
For librarians and teachers: ngchildrensbooks.org
More for kids from National Geographic:
kids.nationalgeographic.com

For information about special discounts for bulk purchases, please contact National Geographic Books Special Sales: ngspecsales@ngs.org

For rights or permissions inquiries, please contact National Geographic Books Subsidiary Rights: ngbookrights@ngs.org

Hardcover ISBN: 978-1-4263-1867-2
Reinforced Library Binding ISBN: 978-1-4263-1868-9

Printed in the United States of America

14/QGT-CML/1